THE FIRST WORLD WAR AT SEA
IN PHOTOGRAPHS

1917

THE FIRST WORLD WAR AT SEA IN PHOTOGRAPHS

1917

PHIL CARRADICE

AMBERLEY

First published 2014

Amberley Publishing
The Hill, Stroud
Gloucestershire, GL5 4EP

www.amberley-books.com

British Library Cataloguing in Publication Data.
A catalogue record for this book is available from the British Library.

ISBN 978 1 4456 2247 7 (print)
ISBN 978 1 4456 2270 5 (ebook)

Typesetting and Origination by Amberley Publishing.
Printed in Great Britain.

Contents

Introduction

By the beginning of 1917, the Royal Navy had fought five major fleet actions – the battles of Coronel, the Falkland Islands, Dogger Bank, Heligoland Bight and Jutland. British ships had also been at the forefront of the Dardanelles Campaign, supporting the Army by shelling Turkish positions, and losing several pre-Dreadnought battleships in the process.

In other theatres of war, losses among smaller craft – cruisers and destroyers, submarines and minesweepers – had been equally great. With many of the ships falling prey to modern weapons such as mines, depth charges and torpedoes, it had become increasingly clear that most losses would not be coming from big fleet encounters but from accidents of chance or individual endeavours on the part of ship commanders.

By 1917 it was also clear that the unglamorous but vital work of protecting merchant shipping was going to become one of the main roles of the Navy in the months and years ahead – and in 1917 there was nothing to say that the war would not continue for several years yet. Since Nelson's days, protecting merchant ships and the vital import of raw materials had always been a part of the Navy's role, but never was it so crucial or so clearly mapped out for all to see.

Despite regular attempts by German forces to disrupt the process, one of the Navy's main jobs was guarding and shepherding the transports, many of them pre-war pleasure steamers, that were ferrying thousands of troops back and forth across the Channel. The disruption of this traffic was a prime objective for the German navy, and protecting the routes to and from France and Belgium was a task that fell to a force known as the Dover Patrol.

By the beginning of 1917 almost 1 million wounded men had been transported back home to Blighty from France, while every day something like 10,000 soldiers were carried across the Channel, in one direction or the other. With Dover and Folkestone acting as the main points of embarkation, this density of traffic meant that the Straits of Dover and the southern part of the North Sea became an increasingly important battleground.

The Dover Patrol was made up of a mixed bag of vessels, from cruisers, destroyers and coastal monitors to minesweepers, drifters and trawlers – along with the odd airship or blimp – and was based at Dover and Dunkirk. Quite early on in the war, it was realised that U-boats – stationed at Zeebrugge and Ostend – were racing through the Straits at night to gain access to the Western Approaches and the Atlantic. The Channel had been mined and was protected by anti-submarine nets but the submarines, operating on the surface, relied on high speed to help them to skim over the nets. As a result, it was decided to illuminate the Channel with high-powered lights.

These illuminations were the invention of Lt-Com. Brock, a member of the famous firework family. Once in operation, the Channel was a glowing mass of light, and U-boats heading for the Atlantic used the waterway at their peril. In future, they would have to make the long and dangerous haul around the north of Scotland in order to reach their hunting grounds. Maintaining the illuminations was another of the tasks of the Dover Patrol and, inevitably, as well as deterring the U-boats it made the ships of the Patrol much more vulnerable to attack from both sea and air.

During the early part of 1917 British and German forces were regularly involved in small ship actions in the Channel and the North Sea. On 17 March a German destroyer raid against shipping in the Straits resulted in the loss of HMS *Paragon* and severe damage to the *Llewellyn*. It was an action that led to reprisals – British coastal motorboats attacked German destroyers off Zeebrugge on 7 April. In this, the first success for the Royal Navy's small coastal craft, the German destroyer G88 was sunk. These are just two small actions that were typical of the work of the Dover Patrol.

Throughout 1917 regular raids against ports on the English coast continued, Southwold and Wangford being attacked on 25 January. Dover was shelled by enemy destroyers in the dark hours before midnight on 21 April (two German destroyers, the G42 and G85, were sunk) and Ramsgate was raided on the 27th of the same month. And so it went on for most of 1917 and 1918.

* * *

Two events impinged greatly on the conduct and course of the war in 1917. In April came the declaration of war on Germany by the USA and six months later, in October, the second, or Bolshevik, revolution erupted in Russia. They were seminal events.

The entry of America into the war had its origins in the now-famed Zimmermann Telegram. On 1 February Germany announced unrestricted submarine warfare, believing that the tactic would quickly starve Britain into surrender.

The downside, however, was that it would also probably impel the USA into the war on the side of the Allies. America, after all, was one of the main suppliers of food and materials to Britain; their shipowners, farmers and businessmen had made a fortune out of 'helping' the beleaguered island nation. To have its ships, its products and its sailors regularly and indiscriminately killed in U-boat attacks – as opposed to the occasional accident or mistake – could only lead to major difficulties.

Believing that the USA was, indeed, on the point of declaring war, and desperate to find allies where she could, Germany reacted. And she reacted badly.

On 16 January Arthur Zimmermann, the German Foreign Minister, took the drastic and, as it soon transpired, fatal step of sending a telegram to Mexico. The telegram stated that Germany and Mexico should 'make war together, make peace together', and promised German help in recovering the lost Mexican territories of Texas, Arizona and New Mexico in return for an alliance.

It was a foolish and forlorn attempt to find friends. There was no possible way that Mexico could have helped Germany in the war, even if her leaders had wanted to. As it was, the Mexican government was desperately embarrassed by the approach, but for Germany, that was only the beginning of the debacle.

Intercepted and decoded by British intelligence officers from Room 40 at the Admiralty, Zimmermann's telegram was passed on to the Americans and duly published by President Woodrow Wilson on 1 March. Deciding to make public the contents of the telegram was a hard decision for Wilson, the arch negotiator. For over two years he had kept America out of the war, hoping to bring all sides to the conference table in a move that would not only aid America's standing in the world but also benefit the economic and political strength of his country.

Despite claims from some quarters that it was all an ingenious British plot, the telegram was genuine enough and, with unrestricted submarine warfare declared, the USA broke off diplomatic relations with Germany.

On 3 February, just a few days after unrestricted submarine warfare began, the American liner *Housatonic* was torpedoed and sunk. Four more American vessels went to the bottom in March.

Woodrow Wilson and the majority of American citizens were outraged, both by the sinkings and by the Zimmermann Telegram. The US Senate, by a majority of eighty-two to six, duly voted for war, a decision that was ratified by the House of Representatives, and on 6 April America declared war on Germany.

* * *

By the beginning of 1917, the empire of the great 'Russian bear' was in the final stages of disintegration. Tsar Nicholas II, the last of the Romanov emperors, ruled over a chaotic society and a downtrodden populace. It was a dictatorship that was as brutal as it was ineffective. After nearly three years of war, food shortages and enormous casualty lists had forced the Russians into a state of near revolution. In February and March that impending sense of doom exploded in a series of strikes, protest meetings and riots.

With the Tsar away at the front there was little his wife, who was in charge during his absence, or his government could do. When Tsar Nicholas, alarmed by reports of civil unrest, tried to return to the capital of Petrograd, railway workers stopped the imperial train and ordered him back to military headquarters. Faced by riot and revolution, Nicholas abdicated on 15 March, ending the Romanov dynasty that had ruled Russia for hundreds of years.

A liberal regime was established under Prince Georgi Lvov but the new government made the mistake of staying in the war. That was not what the Russian people wanted and, fuelled by German money and help, under the leadership of Lenin and Trotsky the left-wing forces of the Bolsheviks began to grow in power and popularity.

The cruiser *Aurora*, the main training ship for the Baltic Fleet, was moored off Petrograd and, with dissatisfaction at the regime growing by the hour, on the night of 25/26 October sailors on board fired a shot at the Winter Palace in the city. Russian sailors were clearly at the forefront of this, the second revolution in Russia, although they were soon to be sacrificed in the bloodletting of the new Bolshevik regime.

It later transpired that the shot from the *Aurora* was actually a blank. It hardly mattered; the shot was the signal for a general uprising. Realising that the game was up, Kerensky, the Provisional Government's leader, slipped out of the city – and from the pages of history – and Lenin and the Bolsheviks came to power.

Lenin immediately began to make overtures of peace. It was the chance for Germany to end the draining and debilitating war on two fronts, and at the Treaty of Brest-Litovsk, signed in March 1918, Russia left the Allies to fight on without her.

* * *

The German U-boat campaign gathered in strength and ferocity as 1917 went on. It was a bleak and bitter war, but a vital one for both sides. Two-thirds of all Britain's food was imported and, despite the privations of a global conflict, the economic livelihood of the country depended on commerce with foreign nations. The rationale for Germany was simple – cut off those food supplies, destroy British trade, sink British ships, and the British Empire would be in dire straits.

April was the peak month for U-boat successes: more than 1 million tons of Allied and neutral shipping was sent to the bottom of the Atlantic. Since the beginning of the war 423 merchant ships heading for Britain had been sunk by the waiting U-boats – almost one ship in every four that left port bound for Britain never returned home. Those were losses that were impossible to sustain. It was clear that unless something was done to restrict the work of the U-boats, Britain could well be starved into surrender. The German strategy of unrestricted submarine warfare was not so far-fetched after all.

There was an answer – convoys. Prime Minister David Lloyd George was strongly in favour of introducing a convoy system, but so-called experts at the Admiralty disagreed. Merchant vessels would never be able to keep to the rigid formation demanded by such a system, they said, and there were simply not enough destroyers or escort vessels to establish a suitable defensive screen.

Lloyd George was not the sort of man to be put off by such arguments. He gathered together his facts and figures, and at a meeting in the Admiralty on 26 April he simply rode roughshod over all the 'expert' opinions. The Prime Minister demanded that a convoy system be put in place. There was no option but to agree.

An experimental convoy was dispatched from Gibraltar on 10 May with the *Mains* and *Rule* as escorts. Everything seemed to go well, the Merchant Navy captains amazing the men at the Admiralty with their ability to keep their ships in close formation.

With the ground seeming to have been wiped from under their feet, an Admiralty convoy committee was set up on 17 May, and seven days later the first transatlantic convoy, escorted by the armed merchant cruiser *Roxburgh*, left America for Britain.

The first of a series of regular convoys sailed from Hampton Roads in Virginia on 2 July and the success was immediate.

Sinkings dropped dramatically and as more and more escort vessels were deployed to protect the convoys, the toll on U-boats gradually increased. It was a close-run thing, however, and the shortage of vital food supplies did finally force the government to introduce food rationing. At one stage there was less than a month's supply of wheat – crucial for making bread – in the country and starvation seemed a real possibility.

It was not until well into 1918 that the U-boat menace was finally quashed but the beginnings of their defeat had been laid the year before. There had been false dawns. An experiment using sea lions in place of submarines had been held in the Gare Loch on the western coast of Scotland in January 1917. Then, in June 1917, experiments with ASDIC as a means of locating submarines underwater were held at Harwich and this, together with the development of effective depth charges, finally gave the men of the escorting ships weapons to hit back at the hidden U-boats.

Convoys were not always totally successful. Merchant ships were still sunk and in the Mediterranean no convoy system existed at all. On 17 October 1917 the German cruisers *Bremse* and *Brummer* managed to intercept a convoy in the Norwegian Sea. They quickly sank the two escorts, *Strongbow* and *Mary Rose*, as the convoy scattered in alarm. In general, however, the establishment of a convoy system was hugely successful.

* * *

Meanwhile, in the wake of their declaration of war, the American navy was beginning to make its presence felt in the Atlantic.

The first detachment of US Navy destroyers arrived at Queenstown in Ireland on 4 May and, under the direct operational command of the Royal Navy, they soon began work escorting convoys to and from the US. A second group arrived on 17 May and a third on 24 May, bringing the total strength of US ships at Queenstown to eighteen.

On 7 December five American battleships – the USS *Delaware*, *Florida*, *New York*, *Texas* and *Wyoming* – arrived at Scapa Flow. Under the command of Rear Admiral Hugh Rodman they formed the 6th Battle Squadron of the Grand Fleet. They were never called upon to fight a fleet action but their mere presence was both a morale booster for the British and a thorn in the side for Germany.

The German High Seas Fleet had, since Jutland, remained largely inactive. To many of the more realistic politicians in Germany, men like the Chancellor, Bethmann-Hollweg, it was crucially important to keep the fleet intact, not as a weapon of war but as a bargaining tool to use with the British should the two nations ever come to the negotiation table. In some quarters such opinions were regarded as defeatist but as 1917 ground relentlessly on and with the tide beginning to turn against the U-boats, it was a factor that could not be ignored.

January

The Cunard liner *Ivernia* was operating as a troopship when, on 1 January 1917, she was torpedoed by U-47 approximately 50 miles south-east of Cape Matapan. The ship sank in an hour but most of the soldiers on board managed to take to the boats or, as this drawing shows, clamber onto one of the *Ivernia*'s life rafts.

This shows one of the lifeboats from the *Ivernia* with soldiers in the water and in the boat. About 120 soldiers were drowned in the sinking; the rest were rescued by HMS *Rifleman* and taken to Crete.

Keeping watch for U-boats from the bridge of an Orient Line ship bound for Australia.

The *Cornwallis*, a Duncan class battleship – similar in design and look to the *Montagu*, which was wrecked on Lundy Island in 1906 – was torpedoed and sunk by U32 on 9 January. She went down 60 miles south-east of Malta and remained afloat long enough for most of her complement of 720 men to abandon ship.

Above: The *Cornwallis* had spent most of her service life in the Mediterranean and was present throughout the Gallipoli Campaign. This rather faded view shows her finally slipping beneath the waves – just fifteen men died in the disaster, all of them killed by the blast from the torpedo.

Left: Navy divers work on the hull of a damaged Allied vessel. Repairing damaged ships and getting them back to sea was an unheralded but important job for dockyard workers and sailors alike.

A British officer is shown here gazing through the periscope of his submarine, searching for enemy ships on the surface. It is a rather fanciful illustration – in reality, the control room of the submarine would have been much more crowded and cramped.

Weapons of war. Torpedoes lie, ready to be launched, in the bow tubes of a British submarine.

A victim of the growing U-boat menace, a steamer, full of fish – said to be worth some £50,000 – is sent to the bottom.

Keeping a sharp lookout for enemy U-boats, British officers stand on the deck of a destroyer and scan the horizon with binoculars.

Hunting U-boats was a task carried out by the Royal Navy and by the Royal Naval Air Service. The dirigible was one of the types of weapons employed by the RNAS. This shows a small dirigible patrolling over the Atlantic. The cupola is open to the elements – bitterly cold when in flight over the Western Approaches – and is actually the fuselage of a BE2 aircraft.

Above: Q-ships – or Mystery Ships, as they were sometimes known – were an effective way of luring U-boats to the surface, when they would be destroyed by the Q-ship's guns. On 14 January the Q-ship *Penshurst* deceived and then sank the U-37 off Cherbourg on the French coast.

Right: Arthur Zimmermann, the German Foreign Minister, originator of the Zimmermann Telegram, which helped bring America into the war on the side of the Allies.

On 25 January the former White Star liner *Laurentic* struck two mines and sank off Loch Swilly. She went down in less than an hour, only 121 of the 475 passengers and crew managing to get into the boats. The *Laurentic* was also carrying about 43 tons of gold ingots – most of it was later recovered by Royal Navy divers but it is estimated that twenty-two gold bars still lie on the seabed.

February

Germany declared unrestricted submarine warfare on 1 February 1917. It was part of the German ideal of 'total war' and was designed to bring Britain to her knees. It was a tactic that very nearly succeeded.

A map showing the areas of the North Atlantic, North Sea and Mediterranean in which the Germans declared that any shipping found would be sunk.

Originally a German ship, first called the *Pickhuben* and then the *Georgia*, the *Housatonic* had been interned in a British port at the outbreak of war. The *Housatonic* was sold to the USA in 1915. In February 1917, just after the German declaration of unrestricted submarine warfare, she was torpedoed and sunk – much to the indignation of the American press.

An example of the kind of marking used to help the commanders of U-boats and other warships to identify neutral shipping. This sign adorned the side of the American Line's SS *St Louis*.

Unrestricted submarine warfare brought America into the war. The Germans knew this was a real possibility but gambled that the policy would starve Britain into surrender before America could bring her forces to bear. The US Army took time to get involved but the American navy was soon battling the U-boats, as this picture shows.

Kapitän-Leutnant Petz, a U-boat commander who claimed to have sunk 51,000 tons of shipping between 6 and 7 February 1917.

A U-boat crew manning the quick-firing gun on the deck of the submarine.

Damaged vessels, abandoned by their crews and left to the elements, sometimes did not sink. Then they became a danger to navigation. This shows one such derelict in the process of being salvaged by an American coastguard cutter.

A British submarine, alongside her depot ship, signals 'MF' to a passing American freighter. The signal 'MF' meant simply 'Reduce speed' – to lessen the risk of collision or swamping.

Lt-Com. Gordon Campbell, commander of the Q-ship *Farnborough*, was awarded the VC for an action on 17 February 1917. Spotting torpedo tracks heading for his ship, Campbell deliberately altered course and allowed the German torpedo to strike the *Farnborough* aft of the engine room bulkhead. A 'panic party' in one of the lifeboats convinced the crew of the U-boat to surface, where she was destroyed by forty-five accurate shells from the British Q-ship. Seriously damaged, the *Farnborough* was towed home and beached.

The German raider *Möwe* had escaped the British blockade at the end of 1915 and in three months managed to sink fifteen Allied ships. Her second cruise was even more successful. Escaping into the Atlantic in December 1916, she sank twenty-five ships before heading for home at the end of February 1917.

About 10.30 a.m. on December 20th, 1916, the raider Möwe held up the French sailing-ship Nantes between Cape Verde and the West Indies.

The Nantes was boarded by two officers, who confiscated her papers and some stores and sent her crew aboard the raider.

At 1.30 a first bomb, fixed aft by the pirates, exploded, and at once the ship took a heavy list to port.

Shortly afterwards a second bomb, fixed forward near the main hatch, exploded, and the ship at once began to go down.

In ten minutes the Nantes went down by the head, watched by her skipper from the bridge of the pirate ship whereon he and his crew were prisoners. These photographs were taken by an American sailor from the St. Theodore, a ship captured by the pirates and used as an auxiliary raider.

PIRACY ON THE HIGH SEAS: SINKING OF THE NANTES BY THE MOWE.

The *Möwe* is shown here in a series of photographs, stopping and then sinking the French sailing ship *Nantes*.

The captain of the *Möwe*, Graf Nikolaus zu Dohna-Schlodien, addresses his crew.

Prisoners from ships sunk by the *Möwe*. By the time she returned to Germany, the *Möwe* was carrying almost 600 prisoners.

THE FIRST WORLD WAR AT SEA
IN PHOTOGRAPHS

1917

The US Navy advertises for men.

'Uphold Our Honour' says the caption on this US Marines recruiting poster.

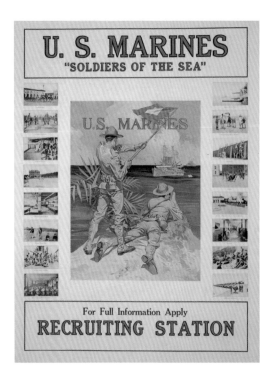

With America in the war, there was a desperate need for men to join the US Marines.

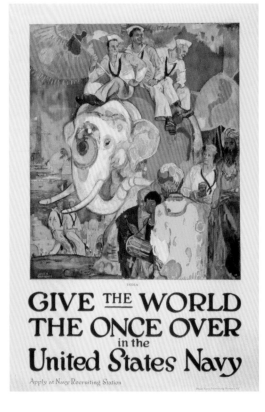

'Give the world the once over,' urges this US Navy poster.

Above: A recruiting poster for the US Navy.

Right: The need to free up men for the fleet was a message picked up early by the US Navy.

Left: The liner *Laconia*, operating as an armed merchant cruiser, was sunk off Ireland in February 1917.

Below: The cruiser *Drake*, named after the great Elizabethan sailor.

The *Cambria*, a White Funnel Fleet paddler, was requisitioned by the Navy to operate as a minesweeper.

U BOAT DEUTSCHLAND, THE FIRST SUBMARINE TO CROSS THE OCEAN, ARRIVING HARBOR JULY 10, 1916, BALTIMORE, MD.

The cargo submarine *Deutschland*, the first submarine to cross the Atlantic.

Regardless of the war, Christmas was still celebrated by both sides, as this German Christmas card shows.

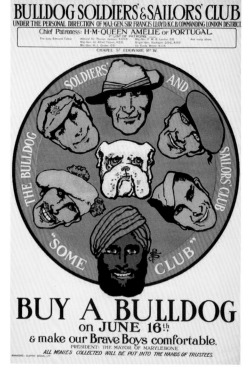

A postcard advertising the Bulldog Soldiers' and Sailors' Club.

Food rationing was introduced as an attempt to beat the German U-boat blockade – a comic British postcard tries to laugh at adversity.

The German battleship *Bayern*.

After the US entered the war, American commanders would attend the conferences on strategy held by senior Allied officers. This photograph shows Admiral Sims, commander of the US Navy's Atlantic Squadron, shaking hands with France's General Nivelle.

A drawing purporting to show one of the 'dirty tricks' carried out by U-boats. Dummy figures in an open boat were supposed to fool Allied ships into stopping to pick up survivors – when they would be torpedoed by the waiting submarine. It is not a really credible story and owes much to the vivid imagination of the copywriters of the time.

Australian soldiers line up in good order to abandon their troopship, which has been torpedoed. Troopships made good targets for the U-boats but, considering the number of Army personnel being moved about the globe, surprisingly few were ever actually sunk.

The 15-inch guns of the battleship *Queen Elizabeth* – for a while the most powerful warship afloat – are fired at the enemy.

'Blinker' Hall, Director of Intelligence Services at the Admiralty. Previously commander of the battlecruiser *Queen Mary* at the Battle of Heligoland Bight, his real contribution to the war was in running Room 40, from where he and his codebreakers provided the Admiralty with a regular stream of information about German tactics and intentions.

A new destroyer takes shape on the stocks in one of Britain's Royal Dockyards. Replacing sunken ships was a vital task.

Above: British destroyers of the Dover Patrol. Sleek and fast ships, the crews of these destroyers soon acquired a glamorous reputation.

Left: An artist's impression of an action in the Channel in which an armed trawler of the Dover Patrol encountered a German U-boat. Despite being badly damaged, the trawler forced the U-boat to submerge and make off.

Sailors at work. Torpedo tubes on board a destroyer of the Dover Patrol are aimed and trained on to the target.

A torpedo leaves its tube, headed towards the target.

Left: A spent torpedo, having missed its target, bobs easily in the water, harmless now – unless a ship should happen to run into it.

Below: Throughout the war, monitors and the heavier ships of the Dover Patrol kept up a regular bombardment of German defensive positions on the Belgian coast. This shows the force in action – a rather romanticised view as, in reality, no attacking ships would be this close to the enemy guns.

Above: A British monitor
– really little more than a heavy
gun platform – opens fire on the
Belgian coast.

Right: A merchant ship is hit
in the stokehold. The fear of a
sudden torpedo did not stop
engineers and stokers carrying
out their duties, but the reality
was that, all too often, men down
in the bowels of the ship had
little or no chance of getting clear
if and when a torpedo struck.

A view showing the control room of a British submarine.

The French liner *Sontay* was torpedoed in May 1917, 100 miles south-east of Malta, en route from Marseille to Salonika. Most of the passengers were rescued but Captain Mages went down with his ship.

The *Sontay* was evacuated in an orderly fashion with no panic. Acting as a troop transport rather than a passenger liner, most of the men on board were French soldiers on their way to take part in the Salonika campaign.

Despite failing to spot the U-boat, an escorting French gunboat came up and managed to pull most of the survivors of the *Sontay* out of the water. This shows the survivors, in the sea and in boats, waiting for rescue.

Allied warships were based in Greek waters from September 1916 to support the Salonika campaign; this photograph shows battleships off the ancient battle site of Salamis.

A German U-boat surrenders to an attacking American ship.

June

An armed
merchant ship
hits back at an
attacking U-boat.

On 7 June construction work on the composite destroyer *Zubian* was completed. She was made up of the forward part of the destroyer *Zulu* and the after part of the *Nubian*, both of which had been damaged in action late in 1916. The *Zubian* became part of the Dover Patrol later in the month, serving with distinction and sinking the U-50. She was sold for scrap in December 1919.

The German cargo-carrying submarine *Deutschland* left Bremen on 14 June, carrying a full hold of cargo, bound for the USA. It was the first time a submarine had been used as a cargo ship. This shows the crew on deck.

The *Deutschland* was a massive submarine, far larger than the average U-boat. Built by private enterprise, she was operated by the North German Line. She made only two cruises as a cargo vessel before being taken over by the German navy and renamed U-155.

River warfare! With much of northern France and Belgium criss-crossed by canals and rivers, the French waterways were used to transport munitions and men, but they were also used by river monitors to bombard enemy positions from Cléry to Saint-Quentin.

Stretcher bearers descending from a hospital barge at a French quayside.

Another view of a hospital barge on one of the French waterways. This time casualties are being brought on board as a nurse and two orderlies watch.

Until the end of the war, transporting troops from Britain to France remained high on the list of priorities as far as the Royal Navy was concerned.

The Navy also carried and protected men going the other way, from the Continent to Britain. This shows a group of German prisoners, under escort, on their way to prison camp in Britain.

Right: Walking wounded enjoy the fresh air on board the ship taking them back across the Channel from France.

Below: Hoisting men on stretchers down from a hospital ship to the quayside for transfer to a train alongside the quay.

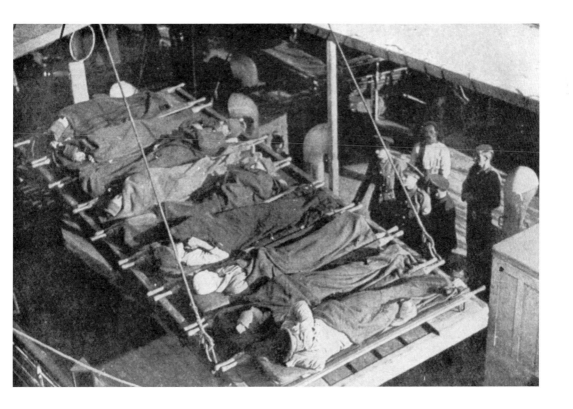

Searchlights from a British battleship hunt for enemy Zeppelins or Gotha bombers.

Right: Belgium had no navy for use in the war, and her marines, like those of Holland and Austria, were a military force used mainly for garrison duties rather than serving at sea. This shows a group of Belgian marines in trenches bordering the North Sea.

Below: With the High Seas Fleet confined to its bases, Germany's marines were also used to man stretches of the trenches along the North Sea coast of Belgium.

In May, 1916, the German Admiralty reported that one of a party of raiding airships had failed to return. This was why.

L7 had been hit by gun fire from H.M. cruisers Phæton and Galatea and finally brought down by a British submarine.

While her broken, blazing hull was disappearing in the waves, her crew swam to the submarine which had dealt the knock-out blow.

They were hauled aboard the submarine and, thankful to be alive, insisted on shaking hands warmly with their humane captors.

DESTRUCTION OF L7 NEAR HORN REEF IN MAY, 1916.

Ein Torpedoboot als Depeschenboot der Flotte.

A German destroyer in heavy seas. Destroyers were built for speed and although they were hardy little vessels, their crews suffered greatly in bad weather.

Opposite: A group of photographs showing the destruction of the Zeppelin L7, which was brought down in the sea near Horn Reef. Shot down by gunfire from the cruisers *Phaeton* and *Galatea*, her crew were picked up by a British submarine.

July

A British airship (or blimp, as the rather cumbersome machines were known) circles the Mediterranean Fleet, keeping a watchful eye for lurking submarines.

An injured sailor is transferred from a destroyer to a large hospital ship, where care, attention and medical aid are more readily available.

British wounded are carried on to a hospital ship in Mesopotamia. The journey for wounded men from the military campaign in the Middle East was usually on board a river transport or gunboat down the River Tigris to the sea, and then by ship to hospital in Egypt.

Another way of getting wounded men aboard hospital ships with a minimum of discomfort: a box-stretcher.

David Lloyd George had become Prime Minister on 7 December 1916. He immediately created a War Council of five men to, effectively, run the war – Arthur Henderson, Andrew Bonar Law, Viscount Milner, Earl Curzon and himself. By the summer of 1917 Lloyd George knew that a system of convoys would have to be introduced if Britain was not to be starved into surrender. He used his power as premier to create exactly that.

Admiral Jellicoe, commander of the Grand Fleet at the Battle of Jutland, was appointed First Sea Lord in December 1916. This shows him outside the gates of the Admiralty in the summer of 1917.

ss ETHELHILDA FIRST STEAMER LIFTED ON PENARTH PONTOON.

Above: A merchantman under repair at Penarth in South Wales. This photograph shows the ship lifted out of the water on a floating pontoon, ideal for repair work on the hull.

Right: A drawing by artist Joseph Pennell showing a gun turret for a super-Dreadnought battleship under construction in a British shipyard.

LOADING BIG GUN - BRITISH NAVY   3176-2

Above: Gunners on the *Ariadne* pose for the photographer.

Opposite above: The battleship *Vanguard* was destroyed by an internal magazine explosion on 9 July. Despite the fact that she was lying close to the shore in Scapa Flow, 804 men were lost.

Opposite below: On 26 July the cruiser *Ariadne*, recently converted into a minelayer, was torpedoed by UC-65 3 miles west of the Royal Sovereign lightship, off Beachy Head.

August

In order to raise money to carry on with the war, one German practice was to carve wooden statues or effigies and then charge people to hammer in a nail. People such as Karl Müller of the *Emden* and Field Marshal Hindenburg were among those who agreed to being so treated. This shows the statue of Admiral Tirpitz at Wilhelmshaven – apparently, huge sums of money were raised by driving nails into this particular effigy.

On 2 August, flying a Sopwith Pup fighter, Squadron Commander E. H. Dunning made the first deck landing on a ship that was under way when he managed to put his machine down on the deck of the *Furious*. It was a seminal moment in naval aviation. This shows Dunning, in the cockpit of his aircraft, being congratulated by sailors. He repeated the feat but was then killed on his third attempt when his Pup was caught in the wind and went over the side. Dunning drowned in his cockpit.

The *Furious*, originally built as a battlecruiser, was fitted with a ramp over her forward gun turrets in order to fly off and land aircraft.

Above: As well as guarding merchant ships, the Royal Navy also transported goods across the Channel. It was hardly glamorous work but it was vital for the war effort. This shows provisions being unloaded at the dock in Calais.

Left: A transport, full of medical supplies and food, arrives at the dockside – much to the delight of the soldiers and civilians who are waiting for her.

A German blockade runner with its decks awash having been shelled by British warships off the coast of German East Africa (now Tanzania).

Holes in the deck of the blockade runner caused by British shellfire.

Left: A large number of the ships that continued to plough the oceans of the world during the war years were actually sailing ships. Steam had not yet totally taken over. The sailing ships were slow-moving, however, and they were easy targets for the U-boats. This shows the sinking of one sailing vessel, torpedoed off the coast of Britain in the North Sea.

Below: A smokescreen, one of many defensive tactics employed by the Navy, is laid by light cruisers.

Above: A close-up view of the secondary armament on one of Britain's warships.

Right: Throughout the war new developments in ship design continued to be implemented as architects, engineers and designers strove to 'outdo' the new warships of the enemy. This shows one of Britain's new submarines, designed and built in the war years.

Above: A deck gun on the *Milazza*.

Opposite: The SS *Milazza*, an Italian bulk carrier, was built in 1916 as the world's largest cargo ship. In August she was torpedoed and sunk by an Austro-Hungarian submarine.

September

An armed trawler and motor launch from the Dover Patrol close in on the spot where a U-boat was hunted down and sunk. The battle over, picking up survivors is now their aim. Rescuing the crews of sunken vessels was one of the main tasks for all crews, regardless of nationality.

An American troopship heads towards Britain. Throughout the latter part of 1917 and early 1918 more and more 'doughboys' began to arrive in Britain and France. The balance of power was swinging towards the Allies.

A British merchantman goes to the bottom as survivors cling to an upturned boat. The enemy submarine lurks ominously in the distance.

Above: Nights were the worst for any sailor afloat in a vast sea and without hope of immediate rescue. Small wonder that some men were driven mad long before rescue.

Opposite above: One of the early depth charges is shown here exploding astern of a hunting escort vessel.

Opposite below: Adrift in a small boat, survivors of most sunken ships faced hours or even days in dreadful conditions. Men froze to death, and sometimes the sea was so rough that their lifeboats were simply overturned and swamped.

October

The cruiser *Drake*, a ship carrying the proudest and most famous name in the Royal Navy, was torpedoed and sunk by the U-79 in the North Channel off the coast of Ireland on 2 October. She had been built at Pembroke Dockyard in West Wales and was the longest ship ever launched in the yards.

The *Drake* sank in shallow water, which enabled most of the crew to abandon ship in safety. Only eighteen lives were lost, most of them in the explosion from the torpedo strike, but her wreck became a navigation hazard. It was hit by a trawler in 1962 and both wrecks were finally demolished in the 1970s.

A memorial service for a fallen comrade on board a German warship.

When Italy finally entered the war on the side of the Allies in May 1915, it meant additional forces for the Allies in the Mediterranean. The Italian Fleet played an important part in keeping the Austrian Fleet 'bottled up' in its Adriatic ports. This photograph (taken in 1917) shows the heavy guns of the Italian battleship *San Marco*.

British warships off the Rock of Gibraltar. The Rock, along with Malta, was the symbol of British power in the Mediterranean.

Keeping the shipping lanes open was the prime task of the Royal Navy – not easy in the days before convoys.

Convoys were not always a guarantee of safety, a fact proved by the German cruisers *Bremse* and *Brummer* on 17 October. They managed to destroy the escorts of a convoy off the Norwegian coast and then sink a number of merchant vessels. This photograph shows the *Bremse* as the last in the line as German ships sail into Scapa Flow at the end of the war.

Above: Italian battleships steaming through the Gulf of Taranto – a calm sea for once. The photograph was taken from the deck of another Italian warship.

Left: The sowing of mines across the entrance to the Adriatic by ships of the Italian navy was one of the success stories of the war. Even though it has never been really acknowledged, these mines helped to restrict the activities of the Austrian Fleet. This shows an Italian minelayer dropping her cargo of mines over the stern into the blue waters of the Adriatic and Mediterranean.

Above: On the night of 25/26 October the second Russian Revolution was started when the cruiser *Aurora* shelled the Winter Palace in Petrograd. The ship is now preserved as a museum in the city of St Petersburg.

Right: Vladimir Ilych Lenin, the leader of the Bolshevik party.

Leon Trotsky, another of the senior Bolsheviks.

November

Allied torpedo boats in a choppy sea. Low and sleek, these tiny craft were wide open to the elements – men were rarely dry, even in good weather, but when the wind blew and the winter storms came hammering in off the Atlantic or the North Sea, conditions on the torpedo boats were dreadful.

Left: Two officers of the RNAS armoured car section pose with a Russian colleague in Romania. Romania had entered the war in August 1916 but at the end of the year, Russian troops entered the country to help the Romanians; the Bolshevik Revolution would end this involvement, leaving the Romanians vulnerable.

Below: British warships at full speed in the North Sea – an imaginative artist's impression published for propaganda purposes.

Admiral Beatty, who became Commander-in-Chief of the Grand Fleet when Jellicoe came ashore and was promoted to the post of First Sea Lord. Even as C-in-C of the Grand Fleet, David Beatty was an impulsive and arrogant man but his public persona made him the 'darling' of the British press and public.

A German mine washed up on the east coast.

December

On the morning of 6 December, the SS *Mont-Blanc*, carrying a load of explosives, was involved in a collision in the harbour at Halifax, Nova Scotia. Approximately twenty minutes later, a fire on board the *Mont-Blanc* caused her cargo to detonate in the largest man-made explosion before the development of nuclear weapons. This photograph shows the damage to houses in Halifax.

The Exposition Building in Halifax, damaged by the explosion of the *Mont-Blanc*.

Some of the dead in Halifax. Some 2,000 people were killed by debris, and in fires and collapsed buildings, following the explosion.

On 7 December, five American battleships joined the Grand Fleet at Scapa Flow. This shows one of them, the USS *Delaware*.

The American squadron was commanded by Rear Admiral Hugh Rodman, an experienced and capable commander.

The USS *Texas*, another of the American ships that made up the 6th Battle Squadron of the Grand Fleet.

The crew of a German U-boat are rescued by the destroyer that has just damaged their vessel. Some courtesy remained with the men fighting the sea war, right to the end of the conflict.

Transporting soldiers, horses, even aircraft across the Channel to France; the work of the Royal Navy was rarely glamorous but was certainly never-ending.

Above: A drifter of the Dover Patrol, one of the workhorses of the Navy whose role was rarely discussed or given much publicity.

Right: Bombardment of the Belgian coast continued throughout the war, not only to support British troops but also because the Admiralty believed – wrongly – that Zeebrugge and Ostend were full of waiting U-boats. The enemy submarines were there but never in the numbers that the Admiralty believed.

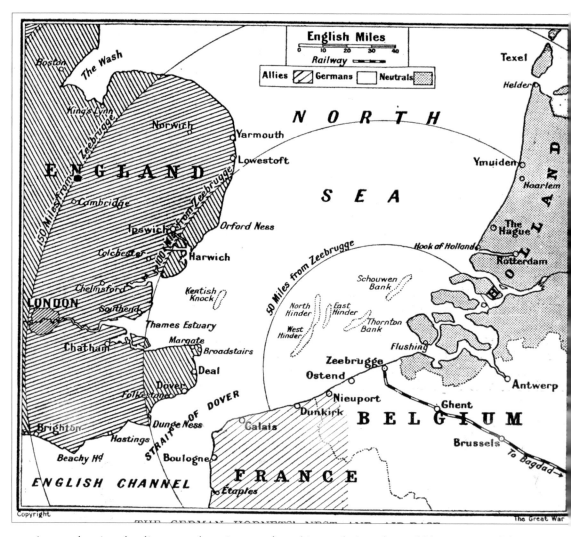

A map showing the distance submarines, surface ships and aircraft would have to travel from Zeebrugge to Britain and the English Channel.

Opposite above: On the night of 15 December the U-62 sank the passenger ship *Formby* of the Clyde Shipping Company as she was sailing across the Irish Sea. The torpedo struck without warning and there were no survivors.

Opposite below: The U-62 struck again, just a few days after sending the *Formby* to the bottom. In the early hours of 17 December another vessel from the Clyde Shipping Company, the *Coningberg*, was also sunk. The ship broke up quickly, within minutes of the torpedo striking, taking eighty-three passengers and crew down with her.

On 21 December, just a few days before Christmas, the paddle steamer/minesweeper *Lady Ismay* was mined and sunk. This photograph shows her in happier times, sailing up the Avon Gorge, decks full of eager trippers who had no idea of what was soon to come.